Split Lip Psalms
Verses in Velvet and Venom

-Hooves-
2025

Printed in the United States of America
First Printing, 2025
ISBN 978-1-949321-30-2

All writings within this book belong to the author.
Cover Art Image by: Ukrainian artist Valeriya Street

A.B.Baird Publishing
66548 Highway 203
La Grande OR, 97850
USA
www.abbairdpublishing.com

dedication

to my wife,
this book isn't yours,
but the hard work beneath it is.

some of these writings rise from us,
from the love you've given me,
from the way you hold my rough edges
like they're worth smoothing.
but most of these pages come from the life
i lived before you,
from the ghosts i had to sit with
so i could finally write them down.

you are the steady breath
behind every late hour,
the quiet belief that kept me working
when memory grew heavy
and the past tried dragging me backward.

the discipline,
the healing,
the new courage to say things out loud,
that's all you.

thank you for being the reason
i could finish
what the old versions of me
never had the strength to start.

Table of Contents

The letter I wish my dead mother could have written me before I, the youngest of 3, had to choose to unplug her; alone.

My sweet boy,

I always knew you'd take the hurt and make it sing. Even when you were small and quiet, watching everything, holding the world too tight in your little fists, I saw it in you.

You had the fire. The tenderness. The kind of heart that didn't flinch from pain, but wrote it down instead.

This book? Split Lip Psalms. It's every sleepless night you thought you were alone. Every bruise you turned into a stanza. Every broken piece you dared to hold up to the light and call beautiful. It's raw. It's loud.

It's you, exactly as I knew you'd be. Full of bite and brilliance. Unapologetically honest. Still standing. Let them read it. Let them feel it. Let them know what it means to keep going when you've got nothing left but a pen and a pulse.

You didn't just survive, baby. You built a voice out of the wreckage. And it sings like velvet and venom.

I'm proud of you.

I'm still with you.

Every page. Every line. Every time you don't think anyone's listening, I am.

Love Always,

Mom

trigger warning (if you insist)

yeah, here it is! the part where i'm supposed to warn you. truth
is, i hate this section. not because i don't care if something hurts
you. but because hurt is part of being human, and these
poems? they just tell the truth.

inside these pages, you'll find:
grief that chews at your heart,
love that burns more than it heals,
addiction in its sunday best,
mental illness with no filter,
mothers who vanish into ash,
fathers who never showed up,
sex without romance,
and romance that doesn't save you.
you'll see loneliness light a cigarette.
you'll see regret pour another glass.
you'll see people try, fail, stay, and leave.

in short: you'll feel something.

and I think that's the fucking point. so, if you're looking for clean
lines, soft endings, or poems that tuck you in; this isn't it. but if
you're here for what's real, for the bruised and bleeding truth of
what it means to survive yourself then turn the page.

just don't say i didn't warn you.

-Hooves-

Book of Velvet
Chapter I

1: don't rush the wreckage

you'll heal,
but it won't be pretty.
it won't be flowers
and sunrise yoga.

it'll be long nights,
ugly mirrors,
and learning to sit eye to eye
with the version of yourself
you never wanted to meet.

don't swallow the lie
that you must hurry because life's a race.
the bastards preaching speed
are usually lost
and too scared
to stop moving.

you don't owe beauty
a single drop.
it's not some trophy
for the well-behaved
and wrinkle-free.

you got time.
take it.

rebuild,
not for them,
not for their soft-focus daydream bullshit,
but for you.
your ruin,
your pace,
your kind of forgotten paradise.

-Hooves-

2: ashes don't hug back

i used to rush through grief
like a junkie late for the fix.
impatient for the scream,
for the wreck,
for something loud enough
to make the silence
stop.

i wanted to drown with the rest of 'em,
gulps,
not sips.
veins full of indigo and scarlet,
turning ghost-white
as i breathed through the sting.

but no one tells you
how the first one wrecks you.
not heartbreak.
not the ones who leave.
but her.

my first goddamn dance partner.
my last line of defense.
she wiped the world off my cheeks
and taught me how to throw a punch with a smile.

she was love without a leash,
laughter without catch,
a teacher who never asked for an apple.
just for me to make it.

and i didn't.
not really.

i let the magic slip
between spilled hours,
let her name spoil in old photo boxes
as yesterday piled up like dirty laundry.

now her spells live in dust.
in the corners i don't sweep.
in the quiet i don't trust.
in the ache that visits

when the whiskey runs dry.

she's smoke now
and all i've got
are ashes that don't hug back.

-Hooves-

3: the decline of the fighter

when i was young,
death wasn't a threat.
he was sport.
a shadow to chase
with split knuckles and scraped knees.
a way to prove
i couldn't be touched.

i'd stare him down
on rooftops and roadsides,
jump from too high,
drive too fast,
take pills like dares,
held cigarettes like oaths.
every bad decision was a bet
that i was immortal
just long enough
to win.

i saw death
the way some boys see fathers,
distant,
but familiar,
and probably beatable.

but now,
now i check locks twice.
i cross streets slower.
i sit in waiting rooms
with bloodwork stuck in my throat
like secrets.

because the older i get,
the more i understand what life costs.

the weight of a quiet morning,
the beauty in breath that doesn't ache,
the way her fingers curl around mine
when she's half-asleep
and doesn't let go.

i used to greet death
like a rival.
now i see him for what he is,
not a test,
but a thief.

and i fear him
not because he's cruel,
but because
he always finishes
what he starts.

-Hooves-

4: no room for fear in a bed built for two

i won't be jealous,
love.
not because i don't think
someone else could want you
hell,
i know a few who do.

but they don't get the 2 a.m. version of you,
tangled in sheets,
breathing like the world's quiet
for once.

you come home
to me.

you fall asleep
with your head against
my chest
and your hand
where it always lands,
right over the place
i keep my stupid,
loud heart.

and as long as that's how we end the night,
i don't give a damn
who smiled at you

i'll only start worrying
if the bed stays
too cold
for too long.
and even then,
i might just
let it freeze.

-Hooves-

5: don't grow old trying to stay clean

i hope you stumble into something wild
before your coffee even cools.
a laugh, a fight,
a kiss that forgets how to wait.

may this year not fuck you as bad
as the last one tried to.
may the sun treat you like an old friend
and not a landlord.

if clouds come,
let them come for the view,
not to drown you.

may the wind shove music
into the torn seams of your bones,
so even when the night bites,
you've still got a rhythm to curse by.

i hope you leave the house
not looking over your shoulder,
but forward,
not for hope,
just something honest.

may you grow, sure,
but don't grow polite.
don't grow silent.
and for the love of whatever's left,
don't grow old pretending to be free.

live it.
messy.
grinning.
with dirt on your hands
and the world still under your fingernails.

-Hooves-

6: for once, the sky didn't fall

we woke up
with mountain air in our lungs
and no messages clawing at our throats.

no sirens,
no headlines
just boots hitting dirt
and hearts that didn't apologize
for beating too loud.

she laughed
like she meant it,
like joy wasn't some rare bird
but a stray
that followed her home anyway.

i wasn't thinking about bills,
or busted dreams,
or all the times i tried to hold love
like a fistful of creek water
and blamed the river
when it slipped through.

not today.

today
we stood stupid and grinning
in a postcard too real to be fake,
wind tugging at our jackets
like a puppy begging to play.

the kind of day
you don't write home about,
you just live it
hard,
loud,
like your bones finally believe
they were built
for more than surviving.

and for once,
the sky didn't fall.
it opened its arms
and said,
"you made it,
you damn beautiful asshole.
don't waste it."

—Hooves—

7: two wheels & teeth

we took the bike out
like we were chasing down some version
of ourselves that still believed
in sunshine
and middle fingers.

she grinned like the world was late with its offering,
like the trees bent back
just to catch a glimpse,
and me?
i bit at her cheek
like joy was meat
and i hadn't eaten in weeks.

the throttle was our only sermon.
no destination,
just the hum of rubber kissing blacktop,
just the curve of her shoulder
under the weight of my hand.

i don't need church when she's laughing like that,
eyes shut,
hat crooked,
one hand on her brim
like she's trying to keep the world from blowing away.

we stopped somewhere
green and godless,
overlooking a lake that looked like it knew secrets
and forgot them
on purpose.

and for once,
the riot behind my eyes
went still.

just her,
just me,
just the wind playing matchmaker between my grin
and her freckled skin.

you can talk about forever,
marble statues,

wedding vows,
all that silk and nonsense,
but give me a bandana,
a busted trail,
and the sound of her laugh in my damn ear.

that's where forever lives.

-Hooves-

8: sleep like a rose (but not the pretty kind)

goodnight,
my love.
may you sleep like a rose,
but not the showroom kind,
not the dethorned ribbon-wrapped fairytale
that sits politely in vases
waiting to die.

no.
i hope you sleep like the stubborn kind,
the ones that outlast homestead shackles
and spit thorns
at anything dumb enough
to get too close.

i hope your dreams are loud,
full of teeth
and soft jazz,
where no one asks you to shrink,
or smile
just to make them feel better.

may your sheets feel like revolution,
your pillow
like a fist unclenched.
let the dark tuck you in without asking questions,
and let the silence know
it has to
earn you.

if the past knocks,
don't answer.
if tomorrow begs,
make it wait.

tonight,
just be.
unapologetic.
unbothered.
unfolding.

sleep like a rose,
petaled but fierce,
resting
with dirt still
under your nails.

-Hooves-

9: wishes in puddles

she didn't dance in the rain
for healing,
or redemption,
or whatever bullshit word
they use these days.

she danced
because it hit her skin
like authenticity.
cold, wet, and
unapologetic.

the past?
it was still burning somewhere
under her ribs.
and the rain?
just steam rising
off old sins.

she didn't leap
she stomped
from puddle to puddle
like they owed her something,
like every splash
was a middle finger
to every bullshit wish
that never came true.

and maybe, just maybe,
she thought
if she stirred them up enough,
those drowned little assholes
might rise
and try again.

-Hooves-

10: good girl

i buried her behind the old shed
the one i used to piss behind when the beer got heavy,
when life felt too full.

she was there for the screaming,
for the cheap women and cheaper paychecks,
she waited at the door
through every blackout sunrise.

i'd come home half-dead,
and she'd just look at me
like maybe i still had a shot.

i named my daughter after my grandmother
because people expect that kind of thing.
but i wish i'd named her
after the only soul who never asked me to change.

i keep thinking
she should've been here
to lick my kid's toes
and bark at shadows like they owed her money.

but all i got
is a patch of dead grass
and a pair of eyes that still wait
when i come home
and no one's there.

-Hooves-

11: where the soft things live

they write epics
about cheekbones and silhouettes,
but none of that
ever made me feel
less alone.

what lies beneath
the kind of beauty
that saves you
ain't loud.

it's tucked
in the soft minutes
between dishes and daylight,
in the way she sighs
in sweatpants
and doesn't know
she's radiant.

there's poetry
in the unbrushed hair,
the chipped mug,
the way her eyes
don't need mascara
to make a man believe
in coming home.

it's never been the glamor.
it's always been
the gravity.

-Hooves-

12: the first one

the porch light burned
like it knew me,
knew the tired shoes
and 3 a.m. silences
i dragged across its floorboards.

that house,
it held my first winter
like a lover with cracked hands,
never perfect,
but damn if it didn't try
to keep me warm.

i left
like you leave anything that mattered,
slow,
with a box of loose screws
and a heart that didn't quite fit in a moving truck.

some places
you don't just untether.
they keep a piece of your gentler self
the one that cried quietly
that tried
again and again to believe
in warmth

tucked behind the plaster walls,
still breathing
when you drive away.

-Hooves-

13: no gods, just granite

some poor bastards
look for calm
in the lull of ocean waves.
not me.
too wet.
too forgiving.

i drag my mess
up where the clouds
hang low
like tired curtains,
stitched between trees older than sin.

up there,
you can almost pretend
you're worth a damn.
walk where the gods once pissed,
olympus or not,
they all bled and bragged the same.

even the broken ones,
the ones with sins still warm in their pockets,
get to stand tall against that stone
and call it sacred.

i climb,
not for glory,
but for silence.
for the wind that doesn't ask
"what have you done."

and when the sky takes me in without question,
i know,
i'm finally
fucking
home.

-Hooves-

14: what your skin forgot, i'll remind it

i'll kiss you
from the scalp where worry lives
to the soles that carried you
into every mistake
that wasn't me.

not for romance,
not for the postcards,
but to remind you
why your goosebumps show up when i do.

ive never drowned in love.
but in you,
i'd sink gladly.
not lip to lip,
that's a cheap gimmick.
i mean
lips to the hollow of your knee,
lips to the stretch marks on your ribs
where time touched you without asking.

i mean
lips to every inch
we forgot to love
when we were too busy
missing each other.

-Hooves-

15: what beauty forgot to mention

they sell it,
in the tik-tok shops,
in instagram filters,
the size two waist,
skin airbrushed into plastic sheen,
as if perfection can be had with a barcode.

but they forgot to mention
beauty's got stretch marks
and doesn't give a damn if you notice.

she quit the contour game,
let her roots grow wild,
wears crow's feet
like medals from a race
she never wanted to run.

she isn't the perfect picture
designed to pull you under.
she's
no more mirrors lined
with lipstick self helps.
no more thigh gaps,
no more trading her comfortability
for compliments.

she's not waiting to be chosen.
she chooses herself,
in the glare of a fridge light,
at midnight,
eating cold noodles
straight from the container.

she's barefoot now
finding grace in
the breath she doesn't suck in,
the joy she doesn't tame
because of laugh lines,
and the love she finds in
her own reflection.

-Hooves-

16: no parades

he did it.
dragged himself
from the mud of boys who never made it,
with calloused hands,
split sole boots
and rage that boiled like coffee forgotten on the stove.

he provided.
endured.
stitched his name into every roof beam,
every dollar stretched beyond dignity.
held his breath through layoffs,
held his tongue through sermons,
held the line
when it frayed his nerves.

they came with their needs,
and he gave,
every time.
even when it meant
breaking things you don't get back,
like time,
like knees,
like the laughter you meant to save for later.

nothing.
no sunset,
no applause.
just a man
who gave up everything
so no one else had to.

-Hooves-

17: now he hears the silence

he used to roar
down some midwest highway
with a woman on the back and money to burn
like i never happened

now he creaks in a recliner
held together by duct tape
and debt,
calling me
like I'm the damn nurse he never earned.

as though bloodline was a contract,
as if the shape of my jaw
gives him license to speak my name
like it still belongs to him
like his last name was a deed
and not a scar.

he says he's lonely.
asks how i've been.
says he wants to "catch up."

catch up to what?

to birthday candles he never lit?
to scraped knees and school plays he missed
chasing women
who couldn't spell our name?

i hear it in his voice now,
the tremble,
the quiet
where his swagger used to be.
that desperate stutter
where pride once punched through the phone.

part of me aches.
yeah.
i'm human.
i see a man
crumbling under the weight of his own choices,
and something healed in me
wants to forgive.

but then i remember:
mom skipping dinner so i could eat.
the eviction notices.
the smell of summers
with no a/c.
his name in my mouth like copper
i couldn't spit out.

i've built a life now.
a real one.
one where my wife doesn't cower when I speak.
where love doesn't arrive riding conditions
like saddle bags strapped to chrome.

he wants time now.
but time's not some bar tab
you settle
when the party ends.

he rode off when it mattered.
burned rubber on goodbye
like it was freedom's anthem.
and now that the road's run out,
and he can't find beauty
in the wild anymore.
he's settling for blood.
for the passenger seat he once left empty
with my name on it.

i think about calling back.
sometimes i even dial.
but the phone just rings
while i stare out the window,
counting all the hours
he never gave.
and every ring
is just another mile
he never crossed.

-Hooves-

18: inherited ruins

i was afraid to fly,
because i never trusted the landing.
that's how it's always been,
clipped wings,
a body tangled in its own weight,
the dirt pretending to be
a kind of mercy.

roses bloomed around me,
but never once bent
their bright heads in my direction.
when they wilted,
i took the hint,
let the ache herd me
back toward the shadow of your door.

the sea was heavy,
all salt and regret,
but i sailed it anyway,
half-drunk on the hope
that redemption wasn't just
a bedtime story
for the broken.

and when i found you,
i stacked fragments like bricks,
hands shaking,
but still trying to build a shelter
out of the wreckage.

this heart,
this bad inheritance,
still beats like a ruined cathedral,
hollow,
but somehow standing.

-Hooves-

Book of Velvet
Chapter II

1: she warmed the parts nothing else could

i used to live in cold corners
the kind of places
where the light couldn't crawl.
where the air bites
and the silence is louder than a beat up engine on a quiet street.

people said it was depression.
i called it wednesday.

then you showed up
with eyes that didn't blink when they saw my mess.
you didn't flinch.
just stood there,
like you belonged in the middle of my wreck.

i never believed in rescues,
still don't.
and you didn't come with sirens,
or rope
or any promise to make it better
you just stayed,
quiet as the ground before spring

you didn't fix me,
thank christ.
you just reminded me
that the fire doesn't always burn everything down.

and now the shadows still hover,
but they don't move.
they know better.
you carved out room where the dark
was too ashamed to fill.

-Hooves-

2: no clock-out for the loved

you want reality?

i can't sit still
without a whip cracking
in my skull.
even in sleep,
i've got a damn clipboard
checking off
what i haven't done,
what i should've done,
what i'll never do right.

2 a.m. and i'm wide-eyed,
choking on to-do lists
because swallowing was never on it.
i can't even take a breath
without weaponizing it
into progress
without sketching the next fucking mountain
i need to summit

because somewhere back there,
behind report cards
and the "i'm so proud of you's",
i learned love was an invoice,
you hand it over
after the job's done.

and i was good at the job.
so i kept performing.
walked the stage with cap and gown
like it meant i mattered
got that college degree
like it was a passport out of shame
i wrecked my lungs cutting firebreaks
like i could walk out of the black unscathed
just to hear someone say
"look at him go"

and now,
i'm married to someone who says
she'll love me no matter what,
but i don't trust it.

not really.
how could i?
when love's always been
conditional.
transactional.
a paycheck i had to earn
with sweat and sleepless nights.

she tells me i'm enough,
but i hear it like a lie you tell a dog
before you close the door.

i don't know how to rest.
i only know
how to win love
by working for it.

so i can't sit in the moment
because the moment's too quiet
and quiet makes space
for that old voice
to say:
"what do you have to offer"

so i run.
and i build.
and i break.
and i call it ambition
because trauma sounds too soft for something this sharp.

but some nights,
when my minds finally quiet enough,
i wonder,
what if i didn't have to?

maybe someday i'll let myself
sit without shame
and still call it
living.

maybe.

but not today.

-Hooves-

3: she doesn't need your hand

she doesn't need saving.
never has.

your magic tricks are a bore to her.
she's seen better twists
in cracked mirrors
and ashtrays.

she lit her own fire
a long time ago.
burned through the pages
while you were still trying to write her in

she doesn't need your song.
your chorus misses
every note
she ever danced to.

you don't have to win her back.
she was never
yours to lose.

she walks like thunder
and doesn't ask permission
to strike.

she's the kind of strong
you don't build,
you survive.

not a muse.
not a damsel.
not an ornament for your shelf of regrets.

she's the woman
you whisper about
when you say
you want more.

and you won't find her
where they told her to stay.

-Hooves-

4: she didn't dress it up

i love her
because she doesn't play pretend.
not like the rest of 'em,
those polished liars
with smiles that fester
from the inside out.

she never feeds me bullshit.
never claps for the scraps
i called talent.
if it stunk,
she said it stunk.
and goddamn,
that kind of honesty felt like
shelter in a world of wolves wearing friendly faces.

she doesn't let me waste
what little time i have
chasing delusions.
no parades, no pity.
just hands,
steady,
real,
the kind that don't shake
just because im broken.

she makes me believe
i'm not ruined,
just cracked.
not some shattered shell
of a man,
just a heart that got kicked
one too many times.

and somehow,
that makes all the difference.

-Hooves-

5: your everyday, the kind i'd bleed for

you knew who i was
with every line i'd lay
not the best parts,
not the polished shit,
but the absolute,
and you stayed anyway.

there's no clean way to love,
no right script,
but damn,
i fell for you everyday.
the way you stir coffee like it matters,
the way your eyes soften when no one's watching.
it made everything else
feel less like a war.

and come morning,
when the world groans awake
and i'm still halfway dreaming.
i reach for you,
every time.
your lips,
your breath,
like something i never earned
but i'll always get to keep.

-Hooves-

6: our kind of harvest

he loved her
like rainfall
on a thirsty field,
with the kind of force
that made her roots
believe again.

his hands washed away
what the others left behind,
every whispered doubt,
every bruise dressed as romance.

and in the orchard of time
where every grape hangs heavy
with some memory,
he reached
only for the sweetest ones.

the ones they made
together.
sunswept,
honest,
imperfect
and still
worth bottling.

he wanted to get lost
on their kind of love.

the kind that didn't ache,
just bloomed.

-Hooves-

7: the stable went empty

i used to have a stable,
full of fill-ins,
half-loved hearts with
daddy issues
and mothers who vanished
like money in a poor man's hands.

i thought i cracked it.
the american dream,
freedom by the hour,
happiness on demand.

she got boring?
switch the channel.
she started to cry?
find the next act.

6 p.m.?
she just clocked out.
2:15 a.m.?
still tanked and lonely,
perfect.

i had one for every flavor of regret.
every room
had its matching silhouette.
and every one of them
looked like a win
in the dark.

but now?
hell, now i'm dusty.
softer in all the places
that used to be sharp.

and i'm in love.
not the bullshit kind,
the one-woman,
talk-too-long-on-a-tuesday kind.
the kind that finds
my fractured ribs,
sits in the dust,
and paints the walls

with all the things
i always needed to hear.

she's it.
she's the whole scene now.
and maybe that's
the newest kink.

monogamy
with bite marks.

but some nights,
just some,
i miss the noise,
the flickering lights,
the always-someone-on-the-line
kinda chaos.

not because it was better.
just because it was louder.
and loneliness
doesn't always leave
when someone stays.

-Hooves-

8: damnation undone in denim

it wasn't fireworks.
no slow-motion orchestras
or grand romantic bullshit.

just you.

black riding jeans,
white crop top cutting the sun
like it owed for its shine.

you turned,
said something about nothing,
and right then,
time held its damn breath.
froze
like it couldn't believe you were real either.

your eyes, ice blue,
but warm
like the kind of liquor
you only sip when you're done ruining things.

and that grin...
salvation,
if salvation had hips
and didn't give a damn about saints.

in that moment,
i stopped being the bastard
who broke hearts for fun.

you didn't save me.
you made me want to save myself.

that's
how you know
it wasn't lust.

lust doesn't stay
after the good part ends.
it doesn't clean your blood off the floor
or ask how long you've been hurting.

but you,
you looked at me
like even my ruin deserved a second act.

and hell,
for the first time,
i believed it too.

-Hooves-

9: on-demand everything

i'm used to life
on demand.

i'm talking
two taps to fuck,
one swipe to vanish.
no names,
no cab fare.
just a body
delivered
like it's got a guarantee.

and her?
she shows up
like pizza,
hot, fast,
apologetic for being five minutes late.
because in this bastardized world
women,
gotta bleed and beg with a smile
just to get picked
like bruised fruit.

they all think
they've got to be fireworks,
they gotta blow themselves to hell
in spark and glitter
even when no one's watching the sky.

but at the heart of it?
i've never been impressed
by fast.

what makes her special
isn't some damn sparkle.
she's not chasing eyes,
she's chasing calm.

the kind of woman who knows
her worth isn't in likes
or lace,
who doesn't need to bare skin
to feel seen.

she stays
because she's done
with cheap exits.

done with being a punchline
in someone else's story.
she doesn't flinch
when the world tells her
"quicker, louder, sexier."

she just lights a cigarette,
mutters "fuck that,"
and leans into the kind of love
that takes its time.

she's the slow burn
in a world full of sparks,
because everything else
is just
a goddamn app.

-Hooves-

10: epiphanies taste like hell and heaven

your shirt's hanging on by a thread,
my hands already greedy,
not undressing,
claiming.
that damp cotton blindfold slides down,
and your breath catches like it knows what's coming.

you sigh like you're giving me something sacred,
but your hips plead their testimony.
they grind slow,
pulling me in
like you've been starving
for this kind of attention.

the room forgets itself.
the walls sweat.
your body hums
and i answer with teeth and tongue,
the heat between your thighs
speaks in tongues
you don't need to translate.

you open,
god, you open,
not soft,
not sweet,
but wild.
raw.
almost otherworldly.

and my mouth?
it doesn't ask permission.
it devours.
epiphanies dripping down your stomach,
messy,
honest,
divine.

and when you moan?
it sounds like forgiveness.

-Hooves-

11: history, not headcount

it was quick,
the way your eyes hit me,
and those hips told the rest of the story
without needing a single damn line.

i drank you
like bottom-shelf whiskey
on a thursday night that felt
like the end of something important.

maybe it was a mistake.
but not the kind
you crawl away from.
the kind you sink into,
knowing damn well
most people
never get that lucky.

you asked me for a number once,
how many.
like it would mean something.

but i never kept count.
who the hell counts when it's real?
when the room's spinning
and you're just trying
to breathe through her name?

lovers aren't trophies.
they're not notches.
they're moments.
they're history.

and you?
you were the kind they write into poems
regret
like gospel.

-Hooves-

12: the lips that didn't move

i've been wrecked by words before,
torn up by syllables dressed as promises,
but yours?
yours never said a thing.

still,
my eyes keep wandering
to that mouth
like a boozehound chasing the rim of a bottle
that already ruined him.

i look at you,
and i go under,
deep,
no rescue in sight,
and lord,
i hope nobody throws a rope.

-Hooves-

13: the angel who stayed in the rain

i once met an angel in the rain,
and she laughed like lightning
had been waiting its whole life
to not be just a flash.

she made me believe
i would never see her again,
because sugar should never stand
through storms this heavy.

she made shame feel holy,
me, hiding beneath an awning,
while she stood bare
to the baptism of gray.

a woman like that,
is worth forgetting every goddamn
reason
i ever ran for cover.

an idea,
fragile and dissolving,
of what is worth melting
to remember.

-Hooves-

14: stitched wrong but still standing

i was built
by a bastard with ambition
and a god complex.
ten fingers, ten toes,
no blueprint,
just bolts and bad guesses.

no heart.
no brain.
just enough spark
to keep me twitching.

they call me soulless,
say i was struck
instead of born.
maybe they're right.

but hell,
what do they know
about being pieced together
with parts that never asked
to belong?

they carry pitchforks
like prayers,
think their fire means something.

but you can't scare
what's already been rejected.
you can't kill
what never felt alive
in the first place.

i don't live to thrive.
i live because i wasn't
given the choice.

and every night,
i look up,
arms open to the storm,
daring the sky
to hit me again.

because maybe
one more bolt
will finally wake the part of me
he forgot to finish

-Hooves-

Book of Venom
Chapter 1

1: slippers in the hallway

cusped in a wave of synapses,
the sweet air of home
wraps me in a quilt of old ghosts
the kind that hum lullabies with cigarette breath
and tucks you in shame
where the warmth should've been
before the heat bill got ignored again.

memory isn't some golden field
it's a fucking minefield you press your luck tiptoeing through.
hoping to remind yourself
you know how to walk through treachery.

and still,
the past paces the hall in slippers too soft to hear
but heavy enough to bow the boards
like some bastard you never invited
but can't make leave.

time?
a blind dog,
staggering through familiar lots,
sniffing at yesterday's garbage
like it's starved with hunger.

i breathe in the dust,
swallow hard,
and call it forgiveness.
because
what else am i gonna call it?

-Hooves-

2: the gravekeeper's gavel

you made it!

don't look so surprised,
everyone ends up here eventually.
some crawling,
some kicking,
some so numb they don't even knock.

but you...
you look like you still believe
you might talk your way out.

don't.

i've watched.
i always watch.

not your resume,
not your attendance record
or the fake smile you wore at baby showers
and funerals.

i watched the way you passed beggars
without blinking.
the way you measured love
by how useful it was.
how you sold your dreams
for something
just shiny enough
to keep the neighbors jealous.

you call it surviving.
i call it cowardice.

did you ever ache for beauty
so bad it crushed your bones?
did you ruin yourself on purpose
just to know how deep
you could feel?

no?

then tell me,
what the hell did you come here with?
there's no reward
for playing it safe.
no prize for staying clean
while life begged you
to roll in the mud and mean something.

i'm not here to punish,
i'm here to weigh.

and you,
my almost-was,
my half-thought,
my missed chance,

you don't get a fire
or a harp.

you get a mirror.
forever.
and the echo
of all the things
you never dared
to be.

-Hooves-

3: lessons, exits, and other bullshit

she asked why
i keep screwing up.
called me out
with that look
that makes a man feel like he's already
halfway to hell.

i poured another drink
and gave her the only story
i had left:

"the harder the lesson,
the more you learn.
but the more bitter you get,
the more bridges
you light up
just to stay warm."

she didn't like that.
most people don't.

they want clean roads.
hallmark endings.
a definition of love
they can post on the fridge.

but me?

i wanted the feeling.
not the frame.
not the rules.
just the damn heat of it.

i hit the road
because she swore
i'd never make it alone.
and maybe she was right.
maybe she knew something
i didn't.

but freedom's got its own scent.
diesel,
gas,
dust,
and something that almost
smells like
home.

these miles are mine now.
the wreckage too.
and if that ain't love,
then i guess
i fell for the wrong damn thing.

again.

-Hooves-

4: the count before the collapse

i sat in the soup
of my own damn routine,
same chair, same coffee gone cold,
same dirty window
i'd been staring out of
since before the world started spoiling.

the rain came like it always does,
a slow, gray bleed
attempting to clean.

so i counted the drops.
every miserable one.
like prayers
i stopped believing in,
like pills
i forgot i already took,
like sins
i refuse to confess.

because i knew,
if i lost count,
if my mind wandered,
if the world slipped back in
like an intoxicated uncle
through an unlocked door.

i'd see it again.

the nothing.
the heavy, sticky,
grinning nothing
i'd spent a whole life
trying not to feel.

and friend,
that's a battle
you don't win.

-Hooves-

5: built on their backs

i sit above these hills,
feet kicked over the edge of a country
stitched together
with someone else's pain.

they were the brave ones.

the ones who taught us how to live
while we taught them
how to die
quietly.

they poured their sweat
into our children,
bled into our brickwork,
rocked our cribs
and
buried our sons.

we paid them back with silence.
with fear
dressed as superiority.

we couldn't stomach the actual.

they were stronger,
smarter,
more human
than the lies we'd written.

still the cops
knock louder
on black doors
than white ones.
still the news forgets
names that are difficult
to pronounce.

suburbia keeps its lawns neat
and its guilt buried
under the begonias.

-Hooves-

6: liquor heat

been thinking
maybe alone's the only place
i don't have to lie.
no fans,
no fixers,
no one asking how i'm holding up
like they wanna hear some bullshit
answer that smells of motor oil and fabrications.

memories?
they've been torched,
acetylene dreams
cut clean through
the good parts
left
only sparks and gunpowder remain

the future?
just a knockoff flame
in a whiskey glass,
dancing dirty
on the edge of hope,
just bright enough
to show me what i'm not.

my veins?
aren't veins anymore.
they're copper pipes
running warm with bourbon and mistakes
holding just enough pressure
to drag my ass forward
one new regret at a time.

i leap from wreck to wreck
just to feel the heat
of the impact.

been cracked open
so long
i don't remember
what unbroken feels like,
maybe i never was.

this ribcage isn't shelter,
but it's what's left.
these hands,
bruised blue with trying,
still open when they shouldn't.
and my heart?
the dumb thing's still limping back
like it knows
no other doors.

-Hooves-

7: no such thing as bad timing, just you

don't blame the damn clock,
it never promised to wait for your hangovers
or your half-healed heart.

the hour never lied.
you just weren't ready.
you were soft,
scared,
still trying to figure out
how not to flinch when it got good.

stop calling it bad timing.
you didn't miss the train,
you were too busy looking in the mirror,
asking why the reflection
still felt like a stranger.

and you,
with your therapy words
and late-night epiphanies,
you keep pinning your failure
on minutes
and seconds
like sorrow ever learned to keep time.

reality is:
you weren't whole enough to hold anything real.
and that's nobody's fault
but yours.

time?
just a ruler
you keep snapping
against your own skin
trying to measure
what you've never had the guts
to become
steadfast
unflinching

alive.

-Hooves-

8: the book i never wanted

i cracked myself open
like a book too eager for its last page,
and there it was,
whole chapters wasted
on ghosts in borrowed faces,
on loves that deserved
to rot in the margins.

their eyes,
so many, so vacant,
all blurred into one
that never truly stayed,
never truly saw me.

you wore your disguises well:
aloof with the morning light,
gentle in the dusk,
but by night
you returned to the same venom,
a liar wrapped in my trust
like it was cheap cloth.

still, i turned the pages,
chasing some violent hope
that ache might bloom,
that ruin at the final line
might rise stubbornly
into a flower sharp enough
to cut.

-Hooves-

9: truth knocks soft

it's a kind of nowhere,
the kind that smells
like dust and forgotten hotels,
known for jack shit
and proud of it.

and maybe that's the draw
a place where nothing's expected
and no one's looking.

truth knocks.
not loud,
just enough to rattle
your last clean thought.

you say,
"not now,
i'm busy searching
for something real."

and so it shrugs,
walks off like it's got
somewhere better to be.

you sit there,
still looking.

truth was five feet away.
you just didn't like
how plain
its face looked.

funny.
but not in the ha-ha kind of way.

-Hooves-

10: you bloomed anyway

you were the kind of beauty
that made men selfish.

and i was no different.
i wanted you
pressed between the pages of my days.
private.
perfect.
picked.

but love doesn't grow
in glass jars
or in rooms with drawn blinds
and one set of eyes.

so i let you be,
out there
in the open.
watched you reach for the sky
without me.

and now every aspiring flower
leans your way.

-Hooves-

11: everybody needs something

i'm the one they call
when the roof leaks like its weeping,
when the dog stiffens
in a bed that smells like him,
when the bills
pile like war medals
and their mind wont stop pacing.

they think i've got answers
like i store them
in the back pocket
of these grease stained jeans,
right next to old receipts
and the crumble of cigarette butts
half smoked through panic.

the phone doesn't ring,
it hunts.
mid meal, mid breakdown, mid breath.
and the needs,
never run dry.
everyone's sinking in their own little storm
and they look at me
like im the raft
they forgot to build.

but nobody asks
what anchors me.
no one worries
how my voice trembles
like a match in the wind
when i say
"i'm fine."
they never hear my gurgling
beneath the surface,
lungs seasoned in salt
gasping
like the sea turned on me, too.

truth is…
i've been scraped clean,
favor by favor,
each "i got you"
a little more emptied out.

and here the kicker
i can't even answer
my own damn questions anymore.
but i've got a voice
that sounds convincing,
so they keep coming.

everybody needs something.
me?
i just want
a quiet room,
and for once,
for the world
to shut the fuck up.

-Hooves-

12: what you never heard

i've got one cigarette left,
dragging fumes
and half-truths
through teeth that forgot
how to lie soft.

you'd never find the bottom
of these words.
not even if you dove in
with god's flashlight
and lungs full of hope.

smoke rings spin like ghosts
against this dark,
curling around phrases
so hollow
they should've caved in by now.

but here's the thing,
my words?
they aren't hollow.
they're just tired.
worn thin
from all the meaning
they've had to carry.

layered like old paint
on broken walls,
even i don't know
what the hell
they're hiding anymore.

they drag me
into corners of my mind
i keep padlocked
from the world.
you'll never get in.
and that's the tragedy.

we still live there,
you and me,
in the haze,
in the silence,
in the parts that didn't burn.

shame we stopped
recognizing each other
before the match ran out.

i think
you'd smile
if you knew
how much of you
still echoes
in my voice,
how even my damn silence
sounds like you
when no one's listening.

-Hooves-

13: the quiet kind of want

he never gave a damn
about the moans,
the sweat,
the lip-biting circus
everyone calls passion.

what he wanted
was the mess after.
your back to his chest, your breath slowing
like an old fan
clicking as you stared at the ceiling.

he wanted
to count the beats
of your soft heart
and know that someday
you'd miss the peace
you once called
him.

and he laughed
the low, bitter kind
at how the world always
traded soul
for skin,
how nobody
remembers
that love isn't loud.

it's patient.
it's still.

like him.

-Hooves-

14: scripted

i was taught
to always introduce myself first
when calling,
part of the systematic construction
of a perfect child.

manners
like mortar
between the bricks of obedience.

even now,
in a world
where caller ID sells your name
before your mouth does,

i wait
for the hello,
then say it anyway,
like i'm still trying to earn
the right
to speak.

-Hooves-

15: choked by the faithful

they say speak softly
and carry a bible.
but all i ever got
was its weight,
pressed against my chest
like inherited guilt,
the kind that stains
before you ever open your eyes.

this place reeks of
hairspray,
control,
and regret
bottled tight under flowered dresses
and sharp sunday shoes.

every "bless your heart"
is a velvet threat.
every smile's
got a leash coiled behind the teeth.
they call it grace,
but it feels like surveillance.

this ain't a bible belt.
it's a noose with a steeple.
cinched so tight you forget what breath ever felt like.
you say "good morning"
and it sounds like a hostage note.

they don't want serenity.
they want
quiet.
they want
folded hands,
downcast eyes,
questions swallowed like bitter wafers.

and if the preacher's got a better car
than the single mom he's baptizing in shame,
well, that's just the lord's provision.

but i see it.
and i'd rather go blind
than pretend i don't.
i'd rather be roadkill
than march one more mile
on the path they paved with
fear,
scripture,
and thinly veiled control.

i want to shout
without a hand reaching for my mouth.
i want to live
without being trimmed to fit someone else's salvation story.

keep your golden gates.

i'll take the fire,
the fallout.
and whatever comes from finally saying it out loud.

at least the burn will be honest.
at least the voice will be mine.

-Hooves-

16: shut the hell up (saves more than prayers)

bite your tongue
before it bites back.
too many words
crack the beams,
turn a home
into a ruin
with a leaky roof
and no one left
to blame
but your damn mouth.

you ever watch
regret
walk in
after you talked too much?
yeah...
it doesn't knock.

sometimes
the brave ones
are the quiet ones
chewing their clarity like stale bread
and swallowing without a toast.

shut it.
not every fire needs gasoline.
let silence haul the freight
for once.

-Hooves-

17: morning had teeth again

i stepped outside
and the air hit different.
that bite
i hadn't missed
but recognized
like an old lover
with a grudge.

the frost kissed me
like it meant it.
sharp.
clean.
the kind of cold
that wakes the lucky
and kills the weak.

-Hooves-

18: they just wanted to dance

i was raised to fear demons.
but now i know,
they preach at pulpits,
smile in photo ops,
and quote scripture while building walls
between love
and survival.

they hide behind
"God's will"
like that absolves them
of blood on the carpet.

somewhere between altar calls and capital gains,
they forgot what it meant
to be human.

the evil ain't in
gay bars.
in the glitter
the drag names
or the way someone loves a body
with the same parts.

it's in the cowardice
of demanding to stay comfortable.
it's in every head turned away
every soft "i just disagree"
every parent who flinches
when their kid says
"i think i'm—"

it's in the silence
that follows.

so if this
feels like fire
under your pew seat,
good.
burn a little.

i hope your shame
smells like burning.

i hope it chokes.
i hope the holy water bites
every time
you chose
the comfort of your faith
over the safety
of someone else's life.

because
i've seen god
and he was in six-inch heels,
kneeling in the street,
calling a stranger "baby girl."

and i'll tell you what,
if that's hell,
then light the match.

—Hooves—

19: the road knows better

come on.
walk this busted road with me.
it's worn smooth
from every poor soul
who thought they'd beat the odds.
who thought maybe
this ache could be bartered
into something softer.

listen to the guy selling hope,
if you must.
he's full of shit,
but it's a prettier lie
than the one you're telling yourself
between drink.
in the quiet gasp
after midnight.

and you'll want his snake oil,
you'll want it real bad,
once your hands start forgetting
what steady ever felt like,
once your knuckles stop bruising from the climb
and just start cracking
under the weight
of how far
you haven't come.

-Hooves-

20: everything we outlived

decay has a low hum to it.
wheezing like old machines
that don't know how to quit.

i never flinched
when death sat beside me though,
i knew the smell
before i had a name for it,
like a body dragged
through decades of open wounds.
reeking of old blood,
broken promises,
and something that used to be hope.

We're meant to leak.
to carry the smell of everything we outlived.
to be proof
that survival isn't the same
as living.

-Hooves-

21: fast food verses for influencers

they call it poetry now,
two lines,
no blood,
just a sigh and a serif font.

"I think of you before I sleep
and that's the nightmare."

and suddenly
the comments flood in
like it's scripture
ripped from the mouth of god himself.
"i feel this."
"this healed me."
"you get it."

what the hell did you get?
a briefcase full of dopamine,
the attention span of a goldfish on benzos?

and a thousand hollow hearts
clapping for something
they didn't even chew.

i've read receipts
that meant more
than these trendy little heartbreaks.

they don't write poems anymore,
they write captions.
fit for reels,
fit for feed,
fit for people too numb
to sit with a sentence longer
than their thumb's patience.

and worst of all?
they profit.

not from honesty.
not from soul.
but from algorithm-approved sadness
cut clean,

bleached sterile,
safe for the soft-hearted
who want to feel deep
without getting wet.

once,
you had to earn pain.
you had to live it.
drag it from the bar floor,
the hospital bed,
the motel sink,
the nights that wore you down to your marrow.

now?
they just whisper a metaphor about rain,
post it by a flower,
and call it grief.

i'm sick of it.
sick of the easy
and the empty.
sick of "poets"
who wouldn't bleed
if you stapled their god damn hearts
to the page.

this isn't gatekeeping.
this is gravekeeping.

and i'll stand here,
shovel in hand,
digging trenches for the words
you
were too clean
to carry.

-Hooves-

22: his hands were never clean

they say he's not looking good.
like depression is something you notice
only when it starts to stink.

but i've seen the guy.
i've watched him drag himself
through morning routines because the habit outweighs the pain.
stood behind him in line
while he stared through the cooler glass
hoping to forget what thirst felt like.
shared a smoke break
where the silence did the talking.

and it's not the eyes,
it's not the slouch,
it's not even the cough that won't quit.

it's just his need for a break
not a lecture,
not a prayer,
not a mother fucking pill,
just a fucking break.

a little help
to scrub the pain out of those hands
he's wrecked his life with.
calloused, cracked,
stained from years of grabbing
at things that never stayed.

he's worn the same guilt
like a second skin.
and no soap's strong enough
to peel that off.

-Hooves-

23: bite the apple, post the fall

they say life's a marathon.
one foot in front of the other.
keep going.
keep breathing.

bullshit.

we're not running for meaning anymore
we're sprinting for attention.
speeding past every real moment
so we can take a blurred picture of it
and pretend it mattered.

every asshole has got a screen now.
tiny, glowing altars
we pray to with our thumbs.
look at me.
like me.
love me.
say i'm beautiful

we used to chase god,
now we chase filters.
we don't live anymore
we just document decay.

and they'll tell you it's progress.
they'll call it connection.
but it's just the same old story
a bite of the apple,
and another fall.

this time
we did it to ourselves.

-Hooves-

Book of Venom
Chapter II

1: only the loved get taken early

you could see it in the twitch of his eye,
that kind of fear that doesn't scream,
just sits there,
boiling slow behind blue glass.
pretty eyes,
but haunted
like motels off the highway.

he lived like a wire
pulled too tight,
always waiting for the snap.
every step dragged him back
to a version of himself he hated
but kept feeding.

he cursed the wrong turns,
the women,
the drinks,
the nights that shook him awake like a jealous god.
told himself,
"this'll be the last sunrise."
said it like a prayer he didn't believe
but needed to come true

thing is,
the world wont keep
the ones it won't miss.
it's the loved ones
that vanish too soon,
the beautiful fuck-ups
with tired hands
and warm hearts
and no idea
how much they mattered.

he should've known.

you don't go early
unless someone
was finally watching.

-Hooves-

2: no crystals for this kind of love

why does everything have to be a goddamn feeling
with a name
and a crystal
and a price tag?

they hand you a rock
telling you it's a cure,
say it hums with "healing energy."
they speak in colors,
green means growth,
blue means tranquility,
red means you're alive.

but i've bled red
on bathroom tiles, borrowed sheets, and hallways walls.
red doesn't mean alive,
it means you haven't died yet.
there's a difference.

they ask me my sign.
scorpio.

"of course!"

suddenly the silence makes sense to them,
the way i vanish
when things get too easy,
the way i love
like a loaded gun
and leave like a prayer nobody said out loud.

they say,
"scorpios feel too much."
like it's my only flaw.
like depth is something you should apologize for.
they say,
"you scare women who want soft things."

and i do.
not out of malice.
not even on purpose.

i don't come soft.
i come with ghost.
i carry the names no else would bury.
i carry myself,
the hardest thing of all.

i don't bring comfort.
i bring clarity.
and clarity burns
when you've only ever known
the gentleness
of a lie.

i don't want to run but
i don't want to stay.
i just want to stop pretending.
this festering thing between us has been nothing but bones
for months.

it's not a relationship anymore
it's a habit.
it's two people sharing a bed with a corpse
and calling it
compromise.

they say it's time for a hunt.
time to find something green.

fuck the green.

the dark is what cradles me
in ways the light never could.

i want silence.
i want lucidity
that doesn't come wrapped in taro cards.

i want out
without asking the stars for permission.

i want out
because it's already over
and i'm just the first one to say it.

-Hooves-

3: planting ugly little truths

most of the time,
i just grab at a word
any damn word
and drag a story out of it by the collar.

maybe it's something i heard,
something i saw,
something i felt
and tried real hard not to.

i don't write to build cathedrals.
i write like a man
digging in dirt
with raw and swollen hands,
just trying
to bury something
or grow it.

it ain't about watching it bloom.
hell, i don't even stick around for that.

i just give the bastard roots
deep ones.
so when it hits a reader,
it doesn't fall over
too easy.

-Hooves-

4: feast on the fools

revenge isn't just bullets or blades.
it's the way i lick my lips
when they think i've lost.

give me the blind world,
the one that traded its sight
for petty debts.

i don't need eyes.
i've got teeth,
tongue,
gut.

and while they prance in righteousness,
i'll be at the table
drinking their wine,
pulling marrow from their bones,
tasting what they never could.

-Hooves-

5: the man who rode away

he called
once every couple seasons,
like a storm with a voice,
talking fast, loud,
bragging on bullshit,
how the cash stacked,
how the harley purred,
how the women lined up
like trophies on a shelf that never needed dusting.

said things like,
"made six figures this year,
got a new bike,
blonde too—hell of a body."

meanwhile
we were microwaving ramen in a busted kitchen,
the lights flickering like they were too tired to stay on.
momma grinding her teeth
while she clipped coupons,
smiling at me so i wouldn't see
how close to breaking she was.

she held up the house on food stamps
and desperation,
walls thin enough to hear your neighbor's grief
through the drywall.

and him?
he was somewhere
chasing younger skin
and chrome dreams,
talking about freedom
like it was something he earned by leaving.

never once
asked how i was doing.
never sent shoes
when mine split open at the soles.
just that voice,
once in a while,
polluting the phone like diesel in clean air.

and i used to think
maybe if i got strong enough,
rich enough,
loud enough,
he'd call to say
"i'm proud."

but all i ever got
was static and swagger.
a father
who rode away
before i even knew
how to spell goodbye.

-Hooves-

6: saint anthony had a sense of humor

they dressed me in white
like fabric blesses bone,
dipped me in holy water
and told me i was clean.

confirmation came,
they said, "choose your patron."
i picked saint anthony,
patron of the lost.

how fitting.
not because i was,
but because i knew i would be.

i prayed like a good kid,
sang hymns like i meant them,
and sat in wooden pews
waiting for something that never came.

before the whispers
became headlines,
before the collars started to stink,
i was already gone.

left the church
the way you leave a bad neighborhood,
quiet, fast,
and with no goodbyes.

and now they say i'm lost.
but if i am,
i chose it.

and somewhere,
i like to think
saint anthony
smirked when i walked out the door,
and muttered,
"attaboy."

-Hooves-

7: matured by hunger

you grow up quick
when the cupboards only echo your fear
and the water
cold
bites like winter,
right to the nerve.

when the same three VHS tapes
become religion,
scratched, flickering sermons
preached by memories
who never needed
a secondhand coat.

your toys are guilt,
your lullaby:
the missing hiss
of unpaid gas lines.

and your mother,
out selling scraps of dignity
just to keep the rent man
from knocking loud.

the worst part?
isn't the hunger.
it's not the shame.
it's watching her
smile through tears
because tonight,
she doesn't have to starve
for you.

-Hooves-

8: they said chase it, just not her

they told me to chase everything.

jobs.
dreams.
that big, wild thing they call purpose.
happiness like it was a goddamn bus you could catch
if you ran hard enough.

"go after it," they barked.
"take it."
"hunt it down."
"don't wait around."

but when it came to love?

nah.
suddenly the rule changed.
you're not supposed to chase her.
you sit.
you wait.
you hope she stumbles over your sorry ass
like a rock in the road.

funny how that works.

why's love the one thing
we're not allowed to want too loud?
too hungry?

what if she never shows?
what if that bastard idea of the right one
was just another trick
to keep us staring at the door
instead of walking through it?

this world loves
to throw riddles at the bleeding.
no real answers,
just more
and more
and more.

and me?
i've gotten used to
never being told anything
that matters.

just more noise
to drown the ache.

-Hooves-

9: not a good guy, just honest

she wanted to give me everything.
so i let her.
took her places she'd only whispered about
in rooms that forgot her name.

then she saw the jar
the one i kept full of hearts,
stacked like poker chips
from every hand i played too hard.

and that was the last time
any of it
felt like sport.

see,
i don't play games anymore.
i don't bluff.
i say what it is like it's my last breath.

some call it reckless,
some call it rude,
but i call it
clean.

because if i go down tonight,
if i drop dead right here.
at least i won't have to lie to whatever comes next.

they say
there aren't good guys anymore.

maybe there never were.
maybe they were always just thieves
traveling from bed to bed,
collecting pieces
like loose change,
leaving wreckage
as souvenirs.

but not me.
not anymore.

i don't steal.
i spill.
and i'll leave you with all of me,
even if
it's too much to carry.

-Hooves-

10: relapse in lipstick

it was 8:18
and my heart
tripped over its own shoelaces.
not the sweet skip of love.
no,
this was the kind of skip
that comes before
the fall.

the kind of skip
that smells like cheap wine
and old perfume
soaked into drywall.

i knew the scent.
relapse hangs thick.
it drips off the ceiling
like old guilt.
and she,
she walked in wearing
every mistake
i'd ever sworn off.

my old fairytale,
now with cracked glass slippers
and a needle full of
"just one more time."

she tasted like yesterday,
aged well enough
to fool me.
and i drank deep.
god, did i drink.

one uncorked bottle
and the whole room spun back to her orbit.
my plans,
my promises,
my hard-earned quiet,
she had them before i could say no.

i called it fate.
but it was a gamble
and the house always wins.

-Hooves-

11: black label and blank pages

i sit at the desk
again.

cheap bourbon in one hand,
regret in the other.
one of them has got to spill,
this paper costs more
than the apology i'm too tired to write on it.

i try to tell what's real,
but the bottle talks louder.
every word i want to say
drowns in the silence of the sips.

the pen stays still.
the glass doesn't.

some nights the only thing that moves
is the level of liquor in the glass
and the weight
in my gut.

so screw the story.
i'll drink.
i'll sit here
and let the ice melt.

that'll be enough for tonight.

-Hooves-

12: wrong turns and whiskey maps

ever look back
and wonder
if turning left
instead of right
would've kept you from bleeding out
on a thursday?

maybe if a, b, and c
hadn't gotten drunk
and slept through the storm,
you'd be in some other version
of your wrecked life
wearing cleaner shoes.

or maybe not.

i chew on that shit
like it's gum
that won't quit.
the missed calls,
the exits i ignored,
the girl who said stay
but didn't mean it.

i walk down the alleys
i should've passed.
i pay tolls
nobody asked me to.
i fix things
just to break 'em again
with better timing.

call it foolish.
call it brave.

i call it
being alive
and dumb enough
to want more.

-Hooves-

13: 20 to the pack

i've been spending
too many nights
staring down
the glowing end
of a cigarette,
like it owes me
answers.

the ember walks slow,
pushed by wind
and bad decisions,
creeping toward my fingers
like everything else that ever mattered.

yeah,
i could quit.
hell, i should've quit
a hundred nights ago.

but who the hell am i
to deny
a little danger?
what's one more burn
on skin that's already a map
of every mistake
i ever loved?

each pack's got
20 stories.
20 tiny deaths
with a punchline.
menthol,
full flavor,
golden turkish,
whatever the poison,
the memory's the same.

smoke curling like a ghost
over parched lips,
another night
i'll lie to myself
and say it's worth it.

who am i
to tell my memories
they shouldn't leave a scar?

sometimes
the hurt's the only proof
you were really there.

-Hooves-

Book of Venom
Chapter III

1: what i spit out

writing it
didn't save me.
just made the pain more organized.

agony scrawled in ink
on used-up napkins,
on bar tabs,
on the backs of hands no one was holding.

what's left
is the flicker before blackout,
a walking bruise
whispering back old names
into smoke rings.
lungs full of static
and breath that taste like
faded dreams.

i didn't want contentment!
i wanted an exit sign that didn't blink.
something to cut the grin off my face.

but instead,
i bled out
every fucking thing
that ever kept me alive.
every last
saving grace.

-Hooves-

2: the closest i get to her now

this pen's the only thing
that still knows her shape.

each loop,
each fucking swirl of cursive,
a memory of her hips,
her breath,
the way she'd trace circles on my chest
back when we still believed
in always.

she said
she hadn't forgotten
what it felt like to sleep by my side.

i told her,
maybe with a little too much bite,
"you made it
real easy to forget
how it felt to have you by mine."

and that was the end of it.
the beginning of the echo.

one time,
she asked,
"if you love me so much,
why don't you ever say my name?"

i wanted to scream it
from every corner of my wrecked chest
but all i said was,
"put your ear here."

she did.
and i swear
for one second,
she heard the beat say everything
my mouth never did.

but that was then.
now,
it's just me
and this pen.

she's still in the ink.
still in the silence
between beats and lines

but never
in my
bed.

-Hooves-

3: ink dries when the soul does

when the pages
come up dry
and the pen
won't bleed,
it's not the world's fault.

it's mine.

means i've been coasting again.
counting days instead of burning them.
means the coke in my whiskey has gone flat
and the sunrises all look like reruns.

i've stopped taking chances,
stopped saying the wrong thing
just
to feel something
crack
inside.

i've let routine
drain the color
from the calendar.

and that's the real death,
not the last breath,
but the stretch of days
where nothing's worth writing down.

so yeah...
maybe it's time
for a night without fences
and a fist full of bad decisions.

because i'd rather wake up with a hangover
than keep going to sleep
empty.

-Hooves-

4: the good ones don't leave, even when they do

the distance got bigger.
the voices faded
into old voicemails and bad dreams.

the light?
it went gray
like a hungover sky that drank too much of
us.

but i meant it
every
damn
word.
not the ones i said out loud,
but the ones i kept in the back of my throat
when everything else
started falling
apart.

you might be gone,
but the mess you left still feels like home.

and i still love you.
not the way poems say it,
but the way whiskey burns going down
slow,
ugly,
and true.

-Hooves-

5: i drink slower now

i sit at a table
that used to be for two.
now it's just me and the silence
chewing on the edge of the bottle.

i've stared at every mirror in this place
hoping to see some version of us that wasn't contorted.
but it's all just me

older,
uglier,
and still holding out like an idiot with a brush
who forgot what color joy was.

i've tried
pills,
people,
bodies whose names I don't remember,
laughter that didn't stick.
nothing fits.

nothing brings back whatever the hell we had
before we broke it
with our own damn hands.

so now
i kill myself slowly
sip
by
sip,
glass after glass,
waiting for something to make sense
that probably
never will.

and i can't die fast.
i've got too many questions
and just enough whiskey to hear the wrong answers
over and over
again.

we fuck up.
that's the one fact i've got.
we fuck up
just enough to learn how much it hurts
to survive.

-Hooves-

6: when stars whisper too loud

i used to talk
about fate
like it was our secret.
something we scribbled in the dark
with our fingers,
bare and stupid
and sure.

i ached for those quiet blueprints,
the ones our souls muttered into being
while the sheets still held
the heat of belief.

but perfect isn't peaceful.
and love?
you stack too much of it on one fragile beam,
it'll crack.
collapse.
burn like hell.

we were a fucking supernova.
too much pull,
too much ache,
too much of everything all at once.

we didn't just love
we collapsed into ourselves
imploding.

and when the smoke cleared,
there was nothing left but echoes
and ash.

and here i am
still standing in the wreckage,
the bones of stars
and memory,
listening
for one last
soft
whisper.

-Hooves-

7: what was left of me

you didn't just break me,
you dropped me like a shot glass off a third-story balcony,
and watched me hit.

i didn't float.
didn't drift.
i slammed into the ground
hard enough to echo off every mirror that won't meet my eyes.

then you walked
right through the mess,
kicking pieces,
grinding shards into the floor like cigarette butts.

i tried
to pull myself back together.
thought maybe i could
be whole again
if i got the edges right.

but turns out
some of me stayed
stuck to you,
buried somewhere
in that cold,
shriveled thing
you call a soul.

so i stopped trying to be
what i was.

i built a spine from the discarded
scraps

created a mosaic.
ugly.
bright.
honest.

and fuck,
it's a sight to behold.

-Hooves-

8: i loved you slow, and it ruined me

i waited.
not out of fear,
not out of pride,
just the usual
sloth
that consumes men
from the inside out.

i had the words.
had 'em for years.
sat on them
like an alcoholic sits on his last dollar,
tight-fisted,
stupid.

so when i finally spit
"i love you,"
the room was already empty.
the light already off.
your perfume was fading
like the rest of my chances.

and today,
i dragged myself to the doctor,
just to check if this heart
was still worth carrying around.

i told him,
"just make sure it's strong enough
to break properly
next time."

because i swear,
next time,
if there is one,
i'll love faster.

even if it kills me.

-Hooves-

9: right before the fall

i think back
and it's always you.
not the good parts,
just the edge of you
sharp,
like secrets you never had the guts to confess.

we were right there,
teetering.

your mouth
a second away from mine.
mine too dumb to stop it.

and i remember thinking,
hell,
maybe this was the dream.
the kind that wakes up
something
missing.

-Hooves-

10: back when i was stupid enough to hope

i used to think about immature things,
like
do you love me
do you want me
are you gonna call
like you said you would.

back when i thought
a heartbeat was a promise
and not just some muscle trying to survive
another shitty day.

i used to wait,
curled up in the glow of a phone
that never rang,
praying to the emoji gods
and voicemail ghosts
for some half-assed proof i mattered.

i was dumb enough
to mistake silence for mystery
and cold shoulders
for some kind of emotional depth.

turns out
it was just
you
loading the next lie.

but yeah,
i used to think
about immature things.
like you.

-Hooves-

11: what we almost were

yeah,
i remember your kiss.
your lips.
your hips.
the way you could quiet the storm
just by breathing
on my neck.

you didn't fix me,
but for a minute
you made the noise
shut up.

i still want the silence you used to bring.
not the holy kind,
just
heartbeat-on-my-back,
hands-in-my-hair,
don't-go-just-yet
kind.

you used to fall asleep
on my chest
like it was
home.

and hell,
for once,
i thought maybe
we meant something.

i let myself believe
in a "this."

and that,
darling,
was the most dangerous thing
i ever did.

-Hooves-

12: ink stained punching bag

my desk's a landfill
half-dead lines,
cheap smokes,
impaired scribbles
i slap it all together
just to feel
like i fucking exist.

i hammer this typewriter
like it stiffed me the rent.
ink bleeding,
whiskey sweating in the glass,
the faster i punch the keys,
the more i think maybe,
just maybe,
the noise will turn into wind,
and that wind
might carry a little piece of me
to you.

i know it's bullshit,
but hell,
a man's gotta believe in something
after he's lost everything.

maybe it hits you
somewhere quiet,
maybe it lands soft
on your shoulder
like a lie you want to believe.

maybe it gets you thinking:
"wonder if that bastard misses me."

and jesus,
if you only knew.

-Hooves-

13: drunk again on the ghost of you

i hope you're listening,
but hell, you never were.

i've been drinking.
that cheap brown validity
that never asks questions
and never lies,
not like you did
with your hands.

time's been spinning me like a bottle
at a backwoods party,
and i've been sunburnt in places
your shadow used to touch.

what matters now?
not much.

i used to carefully count
every
damn
step
between your moods.
measured the thread pulling at my seams,
like knowing the damage
could somehow stop it.

i blamed myself for the dark.
like i invited it in.
like i lit the damn candles
and told the shadows they could stay.

now i drink.
not to numb
but to hold the memory without
trembling.

– Hooves –

14: the pattern of dying slow

i wanted a piece of you.
just a bite.
a scrap.
just a sliver.

but i got the whole mess.
the laughs,
the sighs,
the silence.

then it thinned.
like whiskey over ice.
it was gone.

but hell,
maybe you've still got
one more cigarette's worth of time
to answer a question
that's been sitting in the fridge light
since you left it on.

did you believe the lies?
mine, yours,
the ones we told ourselves
as we pretended growing old
was the same thing
as growing together?

i remember the worst of it.
when the bed felt colder
with two bodies in it.
when we froze,
each of us
shivering alone
under blankets
we used to share like dreams.

we lost it.
whatever it was.
probably during one of those midnight arguments
about dishes
or silence
or how your back faced me
more than your eyes did.

we'd talk
just to kill time.
not to connect,
just to fill the hours
so we didn't hear the sound of the distance
building between us.

you looked at me,
but i swear
you were staring through me
like i was already
gone.

-Hooves-

15: a stranger who knows my name

i sit there
spilling everything i ever buried,
my mother,
my mistakes,
the nights i almost didn't make it back,
while she scrolls her phone
and calls it love.

she tells her friends
i'm "deep"
like it's a fucking compliment.

but when i hand her
the most honest part of me,
inked and shaking,
she doesn't flinch.
doesn't blink.

just says,
"that's nice"

and fuck,
that's worse than a punch.

i don't need her to worship the words,
just give more than nod at the wreckage.

maybe ask
why this one sounded
like a crushing grip around my chest
or why that line tasted
like blood and apology.

but she reads me
like junk mail.

quick skim.
tossed.

silence from strangers?
it's expected.

but silence
from the one who's seen you
naked in all the ways
that don't involve skin?

that's
a different kind of heartbreak.

one you carry
quietly,
like a failed prayer on your tongue,
not sacred,
not hopeful
just the wisp of a scream you couldn't get out.

now i sit
with all that ash in my teeth,
lips stitched shut by every time i mistook
her disinterest
for peace.

because love
shouldn't feel like handing someone your open wound
and watching them
yawn.

-Hooves-

16: more than they could swallow

even as a kid
i knew the world wanted a bite.
knew it'd come for me
with knives and polite smiles.

so i sharpened my bones
and made sure
every damn bite
left a scar.

−Hooves−

17: she never stayed long enough to drown

some women don't drown,
they just walk easy on the waves
as though they softened just for her.

beneath a concrete sky
we drew hope
with broken fingers
into sand
the tide didn't give a damn about.

she took my heart
like it was hers to borrow
and maybe it was.

i held her hand
like a busted lifeline,
like a drunk
grabs anything
not to fall through the night.

but love's a shitty anchor
when one of you
was born to swim.

she untied herself
shrugged off the weight
of everything we built.
turned towards the deep
and dove into the water
like she'd been planning it
the whole time.

what we had
wasn't love.
it was the sound
of her leaving.

again.
always.
again.

-Hooves-

18: what he learned too late

she never sold it.
rather
she bled it.
and every goddamn fool
wanted a sip.
hell, they wanted the bottle.

so they threw it all down
job,
sense,
friends,
whatever
you name it,
just to chase the shape of her in their sleep.

but the dream tangled.
stitched in some silk net that couldn't be
untied.

he set it on a shelf,
like it would stay tender forever,
as if love had no expiration,
as if dust wasn't a kind of death.

he thought time could be reasoned with,
but time doesn't wait.
it devours.

he didn't know
how to swing
without shattering what he meant to protect.
how to bleed
without staining the one clean thing left,

by the time he figured it out,
how to be soft,
how to stay.
she was gone.
left a kiss on the silence and never looked back.

now he's bent like a rusted coat hanger.
chest full of echo.
no heart, just space
where her laugh used to reverberate.

he tells it at the table,
kids staring at their phones.
calls it love.
calls it stupid.
calls it his.

and every night he lies in bed,
talking to ghosts he still thinks
might walk through
the door.

-Hooves-

19: stick, stone, and summer heat

it's so damn hot
the kind of heat that don't just sit,
it leans
like some broke old beer drinker
on your back porch,
refusing to leave
until you've poured out
every last drop of grief.

the air's thick enough to drown in,
and somehow it still finds room
to wring my sadness out
like some sweaty shirt
after three straight days
of begging the sun for mercy
and getting spit on
instead.

i should be glad.
hell, i asked for this.
no more fights.
no more "where the hell are you."
no more pretending.

but i'm mad anyway.
the kind of mad
that wears itself
like wet denim,
clinging,
heavy,
pointless.

you got gone fast.
ran like a mutt
that finally snapped its chain,
not out of hate,
just sick of being kicked
for asking to be loved.

and now here i sit,
in this broiled silence,
my heart
just one more bruised thing

you left behind.
still beating,
still dumb,
still looking at the door
like it owes me an apology

-Hooves-

20: not the same

i asked her,
"what the hell does that mean?"

she just sat there.
no light in the face,
no tremble in the lip.
just blank wood.
a corpse
with good posture.

then her fingers,
the ones that always
kept mine at a distance,
finally touched my face.
not soft,
not warm.
just there.
like closing a book
you never wanted to finish.

the shine had worn off.
she'd seen behind the curtain.
and what was once mystery
was now just maintenance.
cracks in the wall
she could no longer ignore.

her eyes were clearer than ever,
and that's what made it worse.
i wasn't in them anymore.
not even a shadow.
just space.
just goodbye
waiting to be spoken.

her mouth moved.
the same one i used to chase
like a starving man chasing fire.
but now
the words were easy.
not cruel.
just... final.

she said it soft,
but i felt it snap in my chest:

"no reason.
can't explain it.
it's just not the same."

and jesus,
that's the worst way
to lose someone.
not to hate.
not to pain.
just to nothing.

-Hooves-

21: the damn faucet's still dripping

it's loud as hell
that drip from the sink
in a house filled with nothing but
silence
and stale air
and the smell of another wasted night.

the only thing louder than the cockroaches whispering
is my own goddamn breath coming back at me
off a pillowcase i haven't washed
since she left.

the sheets are thin,
but the dirt underneath feels six feet deep.
i lay there,
rerunning the same sheep
like some waylaid shepherd,
begging the reel in my skull to just cut out
and give me
one
decent
night's
sleep.

sometimes,
not often,
but sometimes,
i envy the catholics.

they get to confess,
cry a little,
and walk away forgiven.

me?
i get cornered in my own head until the sun comes up.

they get to drift off,
untouched by ghosts.
i get
whatever the fuck
this is.

-Hooves-

22: i built love with dirty hands

it meant everything
to the nothing i was.
i'd finally wrung love dry.
twisted it, patched it,
bled it out
until i couldn't even tell
what the hell it used to be.

i tossed aside
more lovers than i could name,
each one
thinking they were the fix.

love.
i'd ground that shit
into dust.
too light to hold,
too fine to feel,
disappearing on the breath
of another goodbye.

i kept the scraps.
stitched 'em into something
you might pass as hope.
a crooked crown
made from torn-up promises
and dandelion stems.

i fixed it on my head
like it meant something.
like pain was enough
to earn
something
better.

turns out,
it just cuts
deeper.

-Hooves-

23: what you expect

stop talking.
shut up.
don't twist it into poetry.
don't hand me your guilt wrapped in explanations.

you knew.
you fucking knew
what it would do to me.
and still,
you came home plastered,
lipstick smeared like a confession,
and kissed me
like your mouth wasn't already used up.

you grabbed at me
like you hadn't been fed
just hours before,
but i could smell it,
the sweat,
the cheap perfume,
the betrayal still warm on your skin.

and come morning,
you'll roll over
expecting me still,
warm and waiting,
but i'll be gone,
and all that's left
will be the stench
you dragged in
and the silence
you deserve.

-Hooves-

24: your walls, my weather

i've been standing outside your walls,
the ones you built
for somebody else
who already left.

and i'm soaked.
drenched in the mess of your old heartbreak,
waiting for you to piece together
what's left of your chest
like a barfly
trying to rebuild a stained glass window
with blurred vision.

i know you're scared.
you think i'll see the seams you call scars
and walk.

but listen.
i've got my own busted parts,
stitched up with spit and liquor,
and i didn't drag this far through the mud
just to flinch at yours.

let me in,
and maybe
just maybe
we can compare where we cracked,
trace the broken lines
to the places
we might finally
fit.

not whole.
not perfect.
but goddamn it
together.

-Hooves-

25: i knew better, but jumped anyway

my tongue
still buzzed
from the taste of her.
not lips.
no!
the claws.

she never stayed,
just tore through the room
like a breeze caught in a storm,
a ghost
with wings
and no plans to land.

and still,
i chased it.
the feel of her.
the ache.
that damn whisper that coiled inside me
like a cigarette snuffed out
on tender skin.

i knew better.
fuck,
i knew better.

but something in me ached
like it owed her.

so i jumped.
eyes shut,
heart cracked wide,
off ledges i couldn't even see the end of.

falling.

not for the thrill.
not for a light.

but for the slim,
stupid
chance
that this time,

maybe this time,
she'd catch me
before i
hit.

-Hooves-

26: she never said it, but her body did

i got no right to want you.
but hell,
when did that ever stop
a man like me?

you don't say what i ache to hear,
but i still wake up
draped in your limbs,
your hair in my mouth,
your scent
turning the air into something
damn near holy.

clothes on the floor.
mine, yours,
doesn't matter.
just proof we came undone
in the right order.

you twitch
on my chest,
some small soft dream
dragging you somewhere
i'll never reach.
and i let you go.
again.
and again.

these scraps of morning?
i'd take them all.
hoard them like a gambler
with a pocket full of losing tickets
that still smell like luck.

your heart stole mine
without asking.
danced off
like it never needed rhythm
to ruin me.

that's why i chase the sunrise.
not because i'm hopeful.
hell no,

but because
that brief gold burn
feels like your arms
before the world reminded me
i was never yours to keep.

-Hooves-

27: the wilds of love

the wild of love,
has the shades pulled down and volume up,
the kind of night you don't need to write about
because your bones will always
remember.

her hips spoke in tongues
mine understood,
we kissed like dogs bark
loud, messy,
and full of purpose.

there were no apologies,
just lips,
just sweat,
just fingers tracing maps
only we could read.

she smeared love on my tongue
and i swallowed it like gospel.
we flipped time on its back,
told the clocks to shut the hell up
and let our bodies decide.

no shame.
no lights.
no past to haunt the pillows.
just two beasts
grinning at the ache,
saying:
yes,
this is what it's for.

god never made
anything like this
on purpose.
but we forced the mold anyway.

and when we were done,
we didn't collapse
we conquered.
we held each other
like drinkers

too full of bliss
to be anything else but satisfied.

now that's love.
not the pretty kind.
the kind that howls
not to scare you,
but to remind you
you've been seen,
even in the dark.

-Hooves-

28: the dumbest kind

they say only fools
fall in love.

hell,
then chain me to the word.

i'll trip face-first
into every cracked sidewalk
to see your smile.

i hope
i'm the kind of fool
they write warning labels about.

the kind who doesn't crawl out,
just enjoys the fall
like it was the plan
all along.

-Hooves-

29: lightning doesn't stay

lightning in her bones,
rain in her mouth,
and the kind of glance
that made you forget umbrellas ever existed.

she lit up the dark
like a match to a gas leak,
and yeah,
you knew better,
but still leaned in.

there was magic,
sure.
the kind you crave
when your life's gone gray
and you need a jolt to feel something besides
tired.

but she didn't stay.
magic never does.
she hit,
burned hot,
and vanished before the sheets cooled.

and me?
just some dumb kid clutching a bottle
like it held the answer,
chasing sparks like they'd settle down
and make a home.

they don't.
they scorch,
they split sky,
and they leave you praying
for rain.

-Hooves-

30: she walked like time owed her something

she was the kind of woman
who made you forget
why you ever loved quiet things.

always barefoot,
ankles kissed by a dying sunset,
like she walked out of a painting
and straight into a bar fight.

her lips
not sweet,
not soft,
just full of promises you weren't built to survive.

she didn't say no.
she didn't say yes either.
she just looked at you
and you gave her everything
before she even asked.

a walking scarlet flag,
and every damn lovelorn still ran toward her
like she was the cure.

-Hooves-

31: what she knew before it started

he didn't lie.
he just kissed like maybe tomorrow didn't exist.
soft and slow,
like he was borrowing skin
he had no right to touch.

he wasn't selling forever.
he just meant
tonight,
and he meant it hard.

and she felt it.
the hitch in her breath
when his mouth
brushed her collarbone.
armor slipping
like the battles were over.

she gave in.
not because she believed,
but because she didn't.

because falling into his arms
meant she'd finally feel something
before he disappeared.

and that's the part
that undid her.
the knowing
he'd be gone
and still
choosing
the fall.

-Hooves-

32: one night, no refunds

you looked at me like fire,
and i was winter
with no windows.

your breath hit my neck
like booze on a dry throat.
i damn near salivated
at the sound of your name.

toes curled
like they were praying.
lips?
too busy
choking on moans
to say much.

this wasn't love.
this was survival
with rhythm.
a language made of hipbone confessions
and bitten shoulders.

we didn't talk,
we collided.
skin on skin
like matches and gasoline.

it was filthy.
it was spiritual.
it was art
in the way spilled whiskey sometimes glows
under neon lights.

and when it was over...

no poem,
no painting,
no god
could ever recreate
what we ruined so beautifully
in one night.

-Hooves-

Book of Venom
Chapter IV

1: the fall's the only part worth watching

i was hooked
on the highs.
not for the buzz
but for the fall.

because the drop is the only part
that feels honest.

no pretending.
no smiles.

just gravity doing what people never do
telling the truth without flinching.
i knew the risk.
hell, i counted on it.
something sharp to slice
through the static of another bullshit day
in a never-ending week
of almost
living.

-Hooves-

2: dirt and royalty

i talk about kingdoms,
but i don't want a throne.
i just want your hips pressed into mine
like the world never gave us a damn thing
but sweat
and a shot at something
close to divine.

i don't need a crown.
i need your back arched in a way that says
"you are here.
you made it."

i need you like the field needs the seed,
not for the poetry,
but for the fact
that nothing grows without a mess.
without the digging.
without the breaking
without the moans.

we'll be the rain,
the kind that floods basements
and tears off shingles
but leaves everything green as God.

call it love.
call it madness.
call it whatever the hell you want.
but when we breathe,
we breathe
as we.

-Hooves-

3: wrong number, right voice

just another Thursday,
until the bottle got brave
and the phone lit up at 1:07 a.m.

"UNKNOWN"
flashing like a dare.

i answered,
of course i did,
half-dead, half-drunk.

"Hooooves..."
she slurred through the wires,
dragging my name like a wound
that still itches in places you can't reach.

"you're drunk,"
i said,
pouring another.
"and i'm not drunk enough."

"can i come over?"
she begged.
"just to sleep next to you."
i laughed.
too hard.
"no,"
i said
like a liar
who wanted to mean it.

beside me,
a different girl stirred.
"who was that?"
she asked.

"wrong number,"
i said,
and meant every.
goddamn.
syllable.

-Hooves-

4: fun house gospel

i hate to think that i may be fake.
some knockoff soul
pressed into a face
found in a fun house mirror,
wide-eyed,
warped,
still trying to look whole.

but i am good at pretend.
better than most.
i laugh on cue.
i nod in all the right places.
i've clapped for the wrong people
and kissed with dead nerves like a goddamn professional.

truth is,
sometimes i don't even flinch
when the makeup slips.
i just adjust.
repaint.
slap on some more charm
refit the lie
until even i believe it again.

what a trick,
to vanish
without ever leaving.

-Hooves-

5: a house that lied

trapped in a shit house
built from dying light
and promises scratched into kitchen counters.
faith ran thin,
and every word
stitched into denim
came undone at the knees.

the stairs moaned louder than the people,
and every step reeked of what was lost
not suddenly,
but slow.
creeping.
like time rubbing its elbows on our backs.

the old stories
weren't told anymore,
they just showed up
in crow's feet and bent spines,
etched like bad tattoos
on skin we stopped calling young.

wasn't this life
supposed to be
a thrilling ride?

wasn't there
more
than dying slower
in a house
with broken blinds?

i ran,
fists first,
into every shadow i could find.

but that bastard sun
kept rising
anyway.

-Hooves-

6: yellowbook joints

i was 13
when i choked down my first cheap vodka
like it knew things no one dared to say.
14, burned through a dime-bag
in a busted coke can.
mom caught me
and just passed me another lighter.

she'd tear strips from the yellowbook,
roll me joints fat as guilt,
tuck them behind my ear
like some kinda blessing.

she'd buy my liquor
without the ask,
called it love,
called it making memories.

but what kind of love
teaches a kid
how to pour poison just right?

maybe it wasn't love.
maybe it was her way of saying sorry
for all the ways
she couldn't be a mother.

every day,
a roulette wheel
spun by her moods.

would she wake with the sun,
whistling like it mattered?
or chuck dishes at shadows,
cursing time for not ending last night?

some days she just slept.
cried without trying to hide it.
let the silence talk for her.

and i learned to read her,
better than any damn weatherman,
hopeful for calm,

but always bracing
for the next storm
in her skin.

-Hooves-

7: tape don't hold like it used to

i keep picking through the mess,
trying to stitch something back together with whatever thread's
left
old words, old wounds,
cheap liquor and worse decisions.

the edges curl in on themselves,
worn down like soles after too many walks.
but i keep at it,
because somewhere in the scraps is a version of me
that almost made sense.

these pieces
notes on gas station receipts,
bar tabs signed with half a name
they meant something once.
maybe they still do.
maybe that's the worst part.

now the paper's falling apart,
the ink's smudged to shit,
and this whole damn project of remembering
feels like the most important waste of time
i've ever committed to.

-Hooves-

8: a pact with the ink

when i grab a pen
i know exactly
what i'm doing.
it's not writing,
it's summoning.

every line's an open door
and the ghouls on the other side
still got teeth.

they don't want poems,
they want flesh.

but i write anyway.

-Hooves-

9: she was 76 pounds of gravity

met her at 7:14
in some bar with bad lighting and worse music.
she couldn't have weighed more than 76 pounds
but somehow
she carried the weight of three lifetimes.

i was 24.
too young to be tired,
too stubborn to stop drinking.

she said wedding.
she said dress.
she said something about a son
and a maybe.

it was the kind of story
that leaves bruises
just from hearing it.

and right then
her cane brushed my foot.
made me look at my glass
like it had answers.

what the hell was i doing?
i didn't know.
still don't.

but i ordered another
and by the time it hit the table,
we were in her living room
on a couch
that promised to fit two.

-Hooves-

10: any day's good enough to give up

drinking wednesday's whiskey
from monday's dirty glass,
chasing some friday feeling
that never fucking shows up.

the ice is old.
the burn is familiar.
and the intention?
it left hours ago with the rest of my better judgment.

the calendar says it's tuesday.
but hell what's it matter
when every day feels like sunday morning
with a hangover
and no one waiting for you to wake up.

-Hooves-

11: across the street from paradise

i was five,
living in a florida postcard
they called paradise.
west palm, where the sun
sells lies in every beam.

across the street
was a man with teeth too white,
a daughter my age,
and a son
who never wanted to say much.
they had a house that smiled
but something inside it
stank like spoiled milk.

my parents, bless their blind spots,
trusted him to watch me.
and watch me, he did.

he never touched.
no.
he was smarter than that.
meaner.

he made me and his girl,
play scenes no kid
should even know the words to.

he sat in a chair,
drink in one hand,
rage in the other,
asking why i couldn't "get hard,"
like i was the broken thing.

"you gay?"
he'd spit,
like a five-year-old
should know
what that even means.

i remember the color of the carpet.
a tarnished turquoise,
like the sea when it's in transition.

i remember how the sun kept shining
like it didn't care,
like it agreed.

i never told my parents.
what five-year-old knows how
to describe being ruined
without physical scars?

paradise.
that's what the sign said
as you pulled into the street.

they should've
burned it all
to the damn ground.

−Hooves−

12: hope's a drunk that never leaves

hope is a slippery bastard,
always changing its tune
like a jukebox that skips
when the song's about to get good.

it can hand you a tear worth bottling,
or blow your goddamn life up
before you've had your coffee.

but people?
they keep it like an old dog that bites,
swearing it didn't mean it.

they cradle it
like an ex that finally called back,
acting like it never disappeared
with all their good years.

does hope even know what it's capable of?
how it can crack boulders made of your own history,
dig graves without even picking up a shovel?

maybe hope's more like us than we think.
wandering around,
fucking up,
whispering
"this time will be different."

that's why it sticks,
even when it shouldn't.

even when the door's locked,
the bed's cold,
and the rent's late,
hope sits on the stoop
smoking someone else's last cigarette,
saying: "maybe this time,
i'll get it right."

-Hooves-

13: he should've listened

you were slick
i'll give you that.
you moved that mouth
like you were raised to lie
through come-and-get-me grins.

and damn,
did i fall.
not gracefully,
either,
face-first
into your candy-coated
bullshit.

you didn't just take my hand,
you took the fight,
the backbone,
the sharp parts i needed to survive you.

i ignored
every word
my mother ever said.
and she said plenty.
about girls
like you.

but there i was,
stupid and smiling,
thinking maybe this time
love
would play fair.

it didn't.
it never does.

-Hooves-

14: what the hell's wrong with me?

i don't try.
not really.

okay, maybe i do.
but only in secret.
and never enough
to matter.

every morning
feels like a funeral
with no priest,
just another stiff goodbye
nobody says out loud.

what's wrong with me?
maybe it's you.
maybe it's the whiskey.
maybe it's the way i crawl out of beds
like they're wreckage.

another hangover.
another name i won't remember.
a new pile of clothes
to dodge on the floor.

so what's wrong with me?

i'll tell you
as soon as i crawl out
of this one,
and into the next.

-Hooves-

15: they eat you anyway

the world's crawling with cannibals.
you won't see 'em at noon,
they smile too well.
hide behind job titles
and supermarket greetings.

but after dark
they get hungry.

they knock on your door with compliments.
they nod like neighbors.
they wait for you to flinch.

and once they catch your scent,
your sadness,
your softness
they dig at the old wounds until they split.

they don't need a reason.
just an opening.
just a scar that hasn't sealed right.

they live in your drawers,
your fridge,
your inbox,
your bed.

they show up cold.
they leave you colder.

and still
they come.

-Hooves-

16: they wanted a strip show, i gave 'em teeth

i never asked
to be your damn cartoon,
painted in black and white
like sin and virtue were colors
you could pick off a shelf.

there's beauty in the gray,
the way it bruises,
the way it doesn't beg for applause.

i used to chase it,
that sweet high of losing the reins,
but every crowd
wants you to fall
louder than before.

"Hooves,
why do you still got clothes on?"
they ask,
tongues wagging
like junkyard dogs.

see, they love the show,
the skin,
the shame,
the jokes
that cost more than they're worth.

they call it freedom,
but they never ask
what it costs to undress
in public
when your wounds ain't healed.

every audition a mugging,
every laugh a theft.
i leave behind bones,
nothing but headstones
with punchlines carved in.

i stopped counting them.
started stacking them.
built a little mausoleum
for the pieces they took
when i wasn't looking.

-Hooves-

17: a cigarette and the end of the world

she laid back
like it was her couch
her city
her doomed planet
and lit another cigarette.
smoke curling up like a dare.

he sat there
mouth open,
jaw slacked,
like he'd just watched his beliefs
get undressed.

rules, he realized,
were for men
without women like her.

"you gonna stare,"
she said,
"or
devour me?"

-Hooves-

18: firestarter blues

i've got a hard-on for destruction
but flinch when the fire
gets too close.
i burn the bridge
before my foot's off it,
trip through the flames
like a drunkard in a minefield,
don't care who's coming
from the other side.

i'll toss the match
just to watch it dance,
say it's distance that scares me,
but in my core,
i just love the excuse
to never finish anything.

it's the hit.
the flick.
the fast flash of now
before the sweat
of patience
can even gather.

dreams?
hell, they burn pretty too.
like women who only smile
when they're leaving.

everything's scorched.
tongue's learned to savor the ash.
and even if i claw my way back up
it still tastes
like
hell.

-Hooves-

19: skip the roses

don't put me in a bed of flowers.
i've had enough of soft lies wrapped in thorns.

i don't want petals.
i want flame.
the kind that doesn't ask questions
just does its job.

don't bury me.
burying's for people who
want to come back
and pretend
it didn't end like
this.

burn me down.
all of it.
what we were,
what we said,
the way we left the room like we were just going to the store
and never
came
back.

leave me in the plume.
in the black.
in the same kind of silence
you left me with.

-Hooves-

20: some of us like the dark

midnight comes
and it brings the good stuff.
not silken silence,
but the kind of quiet you can finally breathe in.

the streetlights glare like interrogations.
they want to fix you,
shine you up,
show you the golden path.

but not everyone wants to be found.
some of us got used to the dark.
stitched our sight together with shadows and spit
and called it enough.

you can keep your golden road.
it only shows the cracks we were trying to forget.

no thanks.

i'll take the alley.
i'll take the flicker.
the creak of floorboards as i sneak out the back.
the comfort of not having to pretend
i'm chasing anything
worth catching.

-Hooves-

21: a good goddamn story

they didn't tell it,
they choked on it.
coughed it up
like broken teeth on dirty napkins.

something about
a belt,
a beam,
a body too still
for comfort.

they talked
like their throats were lined
with rust,
like every word was a nail
they had to swallow.

grief didn't weep.
it spat.
it hit the floor
hard
and wet
and stayed there.

and us?
we leaned in like rats.
not for solace,
not for love,
but for the heat.
for the sound of someone else's soul
getting split
down the middle.

because pain that ain't yours tastes cleaner.
like fire
you can watch from the curb.

and this?
this was a five-car pileup
with the bodies still smoking.

we didn't flinch.
we just passed the bottle,
laughed a little too loud,
and said,
"goddamn.
tell it again."

-Hooves-

22: wine for sorrow

i never came to you with mercy,
my hands were vineyards
already starving for rain.

when i hurt you,
it was not accident,
it was hunger.
your tears carried a sweetness
i couldn't resist bottling,
each drop pressed down
like grapes crushed under my heel.

i drank
what i could never name,
swallowed your ache
and called it vintage,
poured your loneliness into a glass
and toasted it as love.

-Hooves-

23: she lit the candles anyway

she wanted me
to believe god was
in her bedsheets.

she kept saying things like
"this feels different,"
and
"you look like someone who's been hurt."

i told her
i just like the way she moans.
she laughed
like she didn't believe me.

her apartment smelled like incense and lies,
and the couch sagged
like it already knew
how the night would end.

i kissed her neck
because it was soft.
i stayed the night
because i didn't feel like driving.

she curled up beside me
like i was something she could fix,
and i stared at the ceiling fan
looking for the answers i thought were mine to keep.

love?
i don't even know
if i'd recognize that asshole
if he knocked on my door
and paid my rent.

-Hooves-

24: they'll read me ink first

on whatever day
they start countin' sins
like pennies dropped in a cracked jar,
i'll be there.
half-blacked out on memory
with skin like old paper
and every mistake etched across my skin
like a jailhouse prayer.

they'll strip us bare,
talk about the image of some god,
but mine had busted knuckles
and never answered the phone.

i'll stand there visible,
tattooed with regret,
spine crooked from the weight of wanting,
while angels whisper gossips
behind smoke.

they'll point,
eyes flickin' like they know the dirt,
wonderin' if my life
was just a bad bet
placed too late.

faith?
i burned through that young
i wagered the embers on women who vanished
and morning that never got better

but i built a cathedral
from the story i was handed,
one tattoo at a time.

and if they wanna judge,
they better read
every goddamn word.

-Hooves-

25: they're just burning things, kid

"aren't they just stars?"

absolutely,
they are
just stars.
giant balls of gas,
millions of miles away,
too dead to care you're crying under 'em.

but sure,
make a wish as they fall to their demise.
tell yourself they're listening.

people always need something
to hang their hope on,
even if it's light
from a thing that's been gone
longer than their father.

each one a graveyard
masquerading as a miracle.

now that's poetry.

-Hooves-

26: cursed with a tongue too hungry

i've got this thing,
not a condition,
not a heartbreak,
just a goddamn itch in the chest,
a hunger that eats me
from the inside
like rats in the basement chewing on wires.

i chew on "i love you" like bad meat,
teeth first,
before the decay sets in,
before time gets its dirty little fingers
on anything tender.

i drown in my own panic,
grab for anything,
a thigh,
a laugh,
a half-poured drink,
a lie in lipstick.

i climb over the wreckage of want,
shove the pretty ones under,
smiles like sharkbait,
trying to float on empty bottles
that used to mean a damn thing.

they call me a leper now,
not safe for land or love,
self-preservation spilled out
like cheap gin
on bar tile.

maybe i need more bottom shelf mercy
bitter enough to blister whatever's still soft in me
just a hit
to hush the ache
and make silence taste tender.

i don't know if it can be fixed.
maybe i'm cursed.
maybe i bit in too early,
too hard.
now all i do is spit up souls
salted with my own
goddamn tears.

-Hooves-

27: let me introduce you

i write under the name Hooves
because it buys me something i can't afford in real life,
failure, without witnesses.

Hooves can say things
that i am expected to swallow.
he can fall apart
loud and messy,
slam his fists on the page
like it owes him something.

and when the guilt comes crawling,
he just flicks the ash,
blames it on the rot in the bottle,
or that split-lipped sky that always looks
like it's about to cry
but never does.

Hooves can overdose on metaphors,
leave every bridge coughing in silence,
grieve a name i haven't spoken since it broke me at 3:14 a.m.
chew on a cigarette
until it's sizzling down the filter,
nuzzle a flask as his hail mary
instead of professing confession,
and no one calls my mother
because no one knows it's me dying

when i write as Hooves,
i crawl into the chaos
i can burn
without taking anyone with me.

my friends don't have to lower their expectations.
they don't have to hold my head up
spoon-feeding me understanding,
sitting with me
watching while the quiet devours my ribs.

my lover doesn't have to pretend she's not scared.
tracing the edges of me
like she's trying to feel for the breaks.

she can sleep beside the name she fell in love with,
not the ghost it writes through

my name stays clean.
my hands stay steady.
even if the words come out shaking
like a man who knows he's swallowing silence,
to write screams.

because Hooves,
Hooves couldn't hold a pen if he tried.
clumsy, thick limbs
wrapped around some cracked bic,
dragging each line across the page like a limp apology
or a slurred confession.

he was never meant to write pretty.
because neither was i.

but between the two of us,
it's Hooves that wades through the filth,
fighting the past i still flinch to name.
Hooves takes the hits
so i can walk straighter.
Hooves howls
so i can speak softer.
Hooves bleeds on the page
so i don't have to paint the walls myself.

because if his words land wrong,
if they fall flat,
if they don't mean a god
damn
thing

it was just Hooves.
not me.

never me.

Joseph

author bio

you made it to the end, which means you already know me
better than most.

this is the part where i'm supposed to offer a tidy biography,
a resume, a hometown, something polished enough to pass
for a clean reason to justify me. but nothing about this book
was tidy, and neither is the life behind it.

here's the truth:
i've lived on every coast of america. i spent years fighting
forest fires and learned the hard way that some things don't
stop burning just because you walk away. now i'm in law
school, trying to make sense of the rules we live by and the
ones we break anyway.

that's the summary they want. but it isn't the story.

the real impression is in these pages, in my guts, my ghosts,
my bad decisions, my better ones, the pieces i don't say out
loud, and in every place something honest slips through.

if you want to understand who i am, look there. not here.
start at page 1, again.

www.ingramcontent.com/pod-product-compliance
Lightning Source LLC
Chambersburg PA
CBHW030829090426
42737CB00009B/929